Handbook
of
Decorative Motifs

Handbook
of
Decorative Motifs

Birthe Koustrup

W. W. Norton & Company
New York • London

Originally published in Danish as:

À LA KELLINGHUSEN
KINESERIER
BORTER & BUKETTER
FOLKEKUNST & FANTASI EUROPA: Idéer til Dekorationer
FLORA & FANTASI: Idéer til Porceloens-maling m. m.

FLORA & FANTASI was also previously published in English as
WILDFLOWER IDEAS FOR CHINA PAINTING

For information about permission to reproduce selections from this book, write to Permissions, W. W. Norton & Company, Inc., 500 Fifth Avenue, New York, NY 10110

Manufacturing by Colorprint Offset
Book design and composition by Ken Gross
Production manager: Leeann Graham

Library of Congress Cataloging-in-Publication Data

Koustrup, Birthe, 1917-
    [Works. English. 2004]
    Handbook of decorative motifs / Birthe Koustrup.
        p.   cm.
    Republication of works originally published in Danish.
    Contents: Plants and flowers — Borders and bouquets —
    Popular art — Chinese ornament — Kellinghusen.
    ISBN 0-393-73148-0.
    1. Decoration and ornament — Themes, motives. I. Title.

NK1535 .K68 A4   2004
758`.42—dc22   2003069118

W. W. Norton & Company, Inc., 500 Fifth Avenue, New York, N.Y. 10110
www.wwnorton.com
W. W. Norton & Company Ltd., Castle House, 75/76 Wells St.,
London W1T 3QT

0 9 8 7 6 5 4 3 2 1

Contents

Introduction

This book is for all those for whom nature is a source of inspiration. My intention is, above all, to help artists and designers in any medium—ceramics, textiles, interior decoration, fine art—use their gifts of observation and their imagination to create new motifs. Neither a how-to manual nor a lesson outline, it is a collection of ideas and examples of ways to design motifs from plants. Some of the motifs are based directly on botanical models; others are elaborations from popular art or exotic locales.

The techniques that I propose are valid for everyone, from beginners to more advanced artists. The important thing is to have the desire to create, to like plants, and to accept a few rules of the "game." I have played it myself for more than forty years, for my own pleasure and in the course of my teachings. I learned my technique from my professor at the School of Applied Arts, Ellen Rimstad, who learned it from Marie Thornam, daughter of my great-grandfather, Christian Thornam, designer, painter, and naturalist engraver, whose masterwork was to perfect and complete the "Danish Flora."

My technique is as simple as it is ancient. You need only to turn to any part of the world to find nature inspiring the language of forms. The best results have been copied and improved upon over the years because, as always, new generations assimilate their own techniques by copying old masters. Note that I use the old sense of the word "copy" to mean "reproduce from a design," and not to trace: you learn nothing by tracing. Copying exercises the eye and the hand, familiarizing you with your model and thereby permitting you to work more freely to exploit the decorative possibilities of forms and colors. It is through this exercise that the imagination plays the game.

If you would like to try, all you need is a supply of paper, a pencil, and some colors. In the following pages, I present my method, but you are free to choose another.

The search for motifs is part of the game and you need not search very far; you can discover them outside your front door, in a garden or a field, at the beach, or even on a balcony. In my opinion, nothing is more agreeable than sitting in a meadow, or along a gully, on a lovely summer day and letting yourself be inspired by the wild flora surrounding you. Among the daisies, forget-me-nots, buttercups, snapdragons, and poppies, I choose a "victim." I always carry a small field guide in my pocket so I can assign a name to my elected flower of the day. Nature is so rich that even the most experienced naturalists can encounter plants while strolling along whose name is unknown to them. While it's not crucial to know the names of flowers in order to be inspired by them, it is nevertheless nice to know with whom one is having the "affair." Moreover, I often find myself wanting to harvest the plant, gathering up its leaves and roots, in order to continue studying it easily from home. I need to be sure, then, that I'm not harvesting a rare or endangered plant.

In addition to the field guide, I also carry a small spade in order to uproot the plant, along with a plastic bag in which to store it. If you are careful to enclose the plant in a damp bag immediately after uprooting it, it will remain fresh for several days; it will last longer if you refrain from harvesting during the warmest hours of the day. Seal the bag tightly with a rubber band. Some plants, however, need to be studied on site, either because they are rare or because no amount of careful treatment will prevent them from wilting.

I use the spade to dig up the longest threads of root possible, on one hand because the roots are as much a source of inspiration as the rest of the plant, but also because plants live longer with their roots attached. So, dig up the plant carefully and shake off any soil that still hangs from the roots before placing it in the bag. Uprooting the plant is almost always necessary, even if you do not want to carry your "victim" home. It's difficult to work while lying on the ground, nose to flower! If you take the plant home, you must immediately put it in a sufficiently large, clean vase filled with water. Most plants will survive in a cool place, provided the water is changed daily. If you follow these precautions, you can begin work whenever you have the time and desire. Eventually you may replant your specimens in the same place from which you uprooted them. They will continue to grow normally for the most part, unless the roots have been allowed to dry out completely. Weeds, of course, last forever!

By studying plants piece by piece—an exercise that can seem brutally mundane—you will train your imagination: separate or regroup the buds, corollas, seeds, berries, and leaves into stylized decorative motifs. How should you arrange the plants? It's a question of your eye, taste, and style. But remember that the simplest decorations are often the most beautiful. In my view, it's crucial to be able to grasp the principal characteristics of the plant again after having drawn it using your imagination.

Before beginning the first sketch, always draw a number of vertical or horizontal lines or concentric circles, depending on the layout you want, using a ruler or compass. Practice drawing as many guidelines as possible, lightly, in pencil, will assure an overall equilibrium to your design. You can then situate the motif in the manner that seems most appropriate for your purpose. The drawings on the following pages demonstrate how you can arrange a small bud to form a frieze or a decorative motif with leaves, stems, pistils, and stamens, spread out seeds of an umbellifer in concentric circles or in a border of semicircles, or plan a radiating design.

Begin with a reproduction that is natural and true to the subject. Some think this step is useless, difficult, and bothersome; I think it is important and necessary because it exercises the eye and the hand, both of which require training. Try to reproduce every detail accurately. Properly draw the stems, flowers, and leaves as they appear in relation to one another. In the beginning, it will be difficult to compose the plant in its entirety, but flowers are patient models. Don't get discouraged; try again. Sooner or later, your patience will be rewarded. Always begin by drawing the principal stem followed by the larger contour lines of its curves, all the way to the roots. Press your pencil lightly to the paper; it's only a sketch. Next, position the flowers, the buds, and the leaves. Hold your model in one hand while you design with the other, or place it in front of you, and remember to always return to the model for comparison. When the sketch is to your liking, add color—watercolors are preferred. Opaque color is not suitable.

Keeping the plant in view, color in small sections beginning at the top of the sketch to avoid smudging the watercolors with your hand. Begin with light colors—blended tones—and allow them to dry before applying one or two more layers of color, particularly on the areas of the model in shadow. It's important to identify the placement of the shadows from the beginning because they will enliven and give relief to the overall design.

Green dominates the majority of floral studies. Your work will be to find nuances of green that aren't available on the palette, but are obtainable by mixing yellow and blue with, sometimes, a bit of reddish-violet. Here, again, begin with light green colors and add another layer after the first has dried, to avoid weighing down the image.

If you are unsuccessful in your design, don't despair. Persevere, focusing on one part of the plant only—a branch or a flower, perhaps. Regardless of the degree of success, this work will give you a glimpse into the structure of plants, a knowledge that will serve you well as you proceed.

Some of your efforts may deserve framing and hanging on the wall; others will only partially satisfy you. But keep even these at least a little while, and preferably longer, in a file or archive: sometimes one successful detail is enough to serve as a point of departure for a new design. Little by little, you can build up a collection of drawings to dip into for ideas before setting off on another project. You will find that it is much more pleasurable to use your own creations than to copy those of others.

The motifs in the first two sections of this book are based on directly observed plants, drawn either singly from specimens or in arrangements, such as garlands and bouquets. In some I have purposely left the guidelines in order to more clearly illustrate the structure of the design. The third and fourth groups of motifs come from farther afield: they are adaptations from European folk art and Asian themes. The idea to use these sources came to me spontaneously and provided a rich source of inspiration for work during the winter, botany being reserved for the summer season. These illustrations are not, with a few exceptions, exact copies, but rather my interpretations of traditional motifs. For years I have never visited a museum or an exhibit without bringing my sketchbook along. I always have it within reach, whether I am reading a book, a magazine, or watching television, thereby capturing the smallest details of interest. Sometimes it is impossible to capture a passing detail—the embroidery on the blouse of a folkloric dancer, a façade glimpsed from a car. Therefore, I take photographs! There are also postcards, museum catalogs, and many beautiful books that permit you to work from the comfort of home.

Use your gift of observation and your imagination to create new motifs: it is up to you to search and play.

Enjoy!

Chapter One

Plants
and
Flowers

The illustrations in this chapter are works inspired by thirty-five plants, flowers, and bushes. The captions give the common and Latin names and a brief description of the plants, as well as the areas and times of year during which they can be found; of course, some of these may not grow where you live, or may flourish at different times. No matter: use these freely for inspiration, and choose your own models from what is available to you. The order of the illustrations follows the seasons.

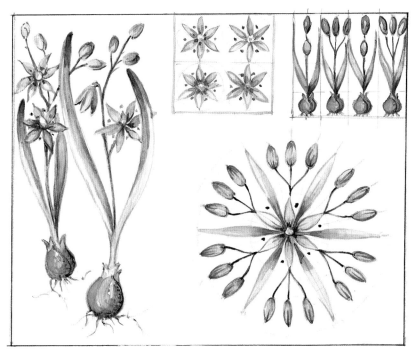

Top: winter aconite (*Eranthis hiemalis*); bottom: squill (*Scilla* spp.). These plants announce the arrival of spring in gardens. Winter aconite sprouts from the earth before the snow has completely disappeared and flowers in March. By April, the plant has already lost its flowers, but the leaves are interesting and wilt, in turn, in the summer. Squill is a bulb plant 4 to 8 in (10 to 12 cm) long, from the *Liliaceae* family, and flowers in April. A wild species of it can be found in Europe; other species are cultivated.

Coltsfoot (*Tussilago farfara*). Coltsfoot is one of the first wild flowers to bloom. In March, its yellow corollas illuminate the still-bare meadows, clayey hillsides, and ditches. The leaves don't appear until after it flowers. The white, downy seeds resemble those of the dandelion and, in fact,

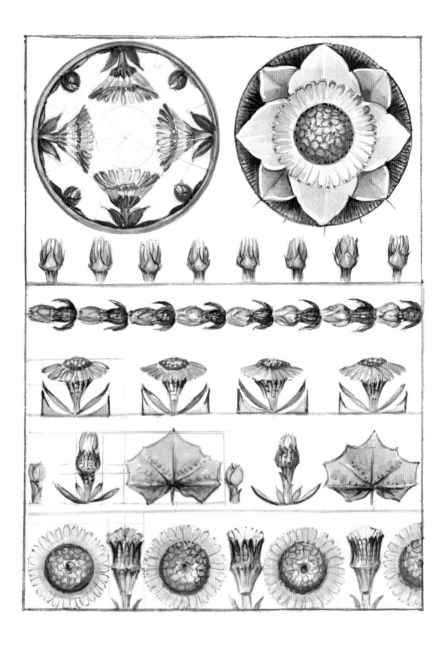

many people confuse these two plants, which belong to the same large composite family—an inexhaustible source of inspiration. A medicinal plant, the leaves and roots of coltsfoot are still used today to prevent all sorts of maladies, particularly a cough.

Field horsetail (*Equisetum arvense*). Horsetail belongs to the cryptogam family, which covered much of the earth with its foliage during the carboniferous period. It grows in clayey soils on hillsides and along roads. From April to May appear short-lived "ears" that are yellowish brown in

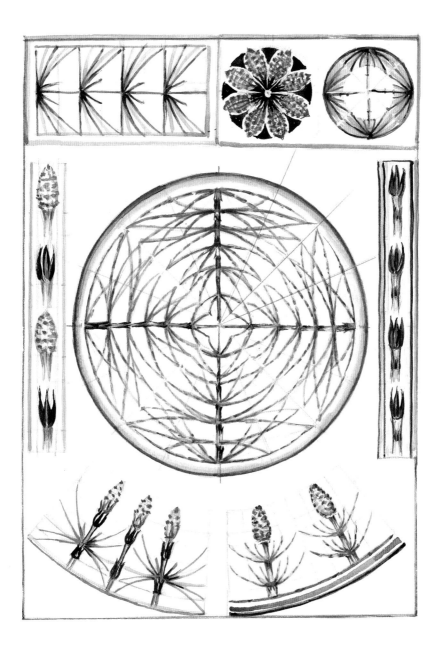

color and carry spores. Then, green branches grow (left), reaching a height of 12 in (30 cm). A plant favored by witches and herbalists, horsetail became a health supplement used in herbal tea.

Yellow anemone (*Anemone ranunculoides*). This rather rare anemone can be found growing in the moist soils of forests. It often carries two or three flowers per stem, and the leaves are rounded. It's important to replant the anemone immediately after use.

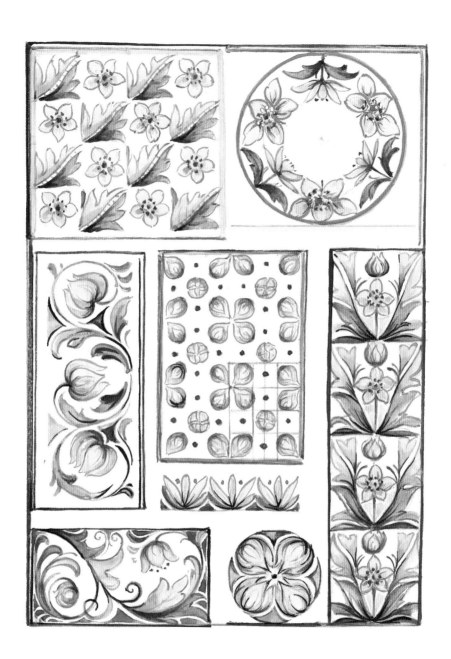

Liverwort (*Anemone hepatica*) and wood anemone (*Anemone nemorosa*). Anemones belong to the *Ranunculaceae* family and grow from March to May. Liverwort grows on clayey, limestone soil in forests, but acclimates well to gardens where it can be transplanted. Its Latin name, meaning "liver," comes from the shape of its leaves. Years ago the plant was used to

treat liver disease, but its use is not advisable today: most anemones are toxic. The wood anemone blooms in April, before the full foliage of forest trees shades the underbrush, which the anemone speckles with thousands of white and rose-colored stars. Unfortunately, it wilts rather quickly in vases, making it futile to gather in a large quantity.

Marsh marigold (*Caltha palustris*). Like the anemone, the marsh marigold belongs to the *Ranunculaceae* family. It thrives in water or very moist soil. Its lively yellow flowers, reaching a height of 6 to 12 in (15 to

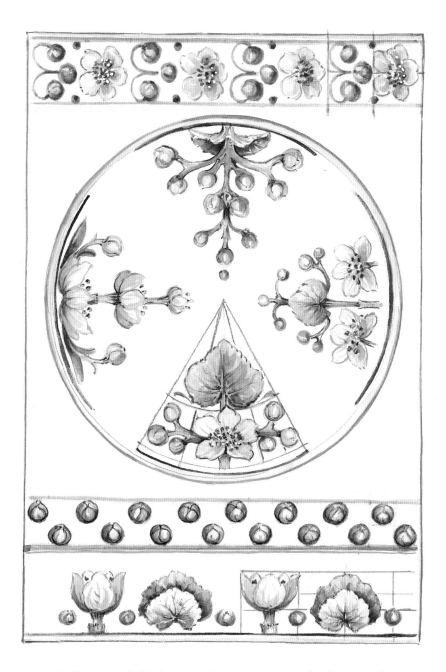

30 cm), illuminate fields from April to May. The seeds of the marsh marigold cover the surface of water and spread to other wet areas. The plant is toxic.

Forget-me-nots (*Myosotis palustris*). Forget-me-nots bloom from May to August in meadows and along riverbanks. The leaves are rough (earning the name "mouse's ear" in certain regions). The plant measures 6 to 16 in

(15 to 40 cm) in height. New buds and flowers are often pink, before turning sky-blue. Among the numerous species that exist, those that are found in meadows have the largest flowers.

Money plant (*Lunaria annua*). The money plant, which belongs to the *Cruciferae* family, grows wild in certain regions, but an improved species is also cultivated in gardens, where it blossoms in June. The seeds that

grow in a silver "envelope" are the most interesting aspect of the plant. The plant survives in gardens well into the winter and is used in dried flower arrangements.

Scarlet pimpernel (*Anagallis arvensis*). Belonging to the *Primulaceae* family, the scarlet pimpernel measures 2 to 8 in (5 to 20 cm) high and blooms throughout the summer. A common weed in cultivated gardens,

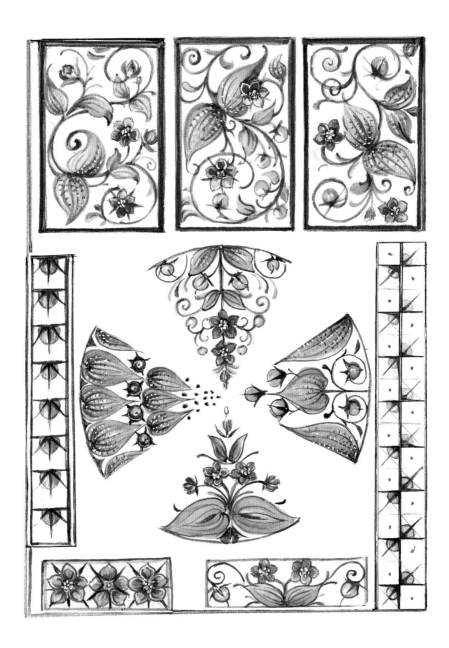

its petals close up when it is going to rain, thereby serving as a barometer for gardeners.

Japanese flowering quince (*Chaenomeles japonica*). This flower comes from Asia and embellishes a number of parks and gardens. It blossoms in April and May and is covered with corollas of a very nuanced, brick-red

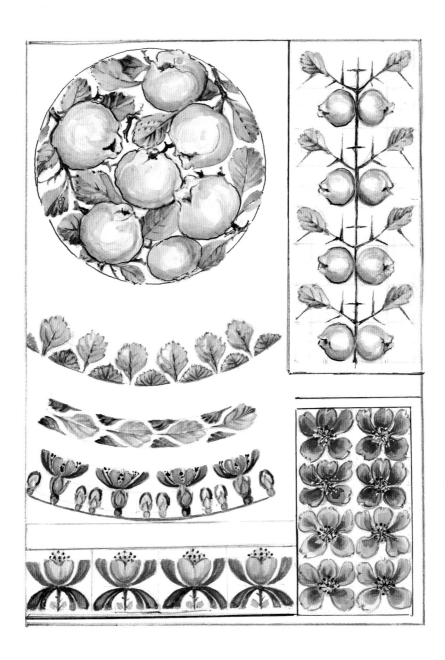

color. Its fruits, which should be harvested as late in the season as possible, but before the first frost, are edible, either stewed or made into jam.

Bladder campion (*Silene vulgaris*). Cousin to the carnation, this flower grows along roadsides and on semi-arid terrain. The plant measures up to 26 in (65 cm) in height and blooms from June to August. The name comes from its balloon-like calyx filled with air, as well as the snapping

sound it makes when pressed between two fingers. Night butterflies are responsible for its fertilization. Bladder campion is a medicinal plant whose roots contain a substance that, when mixed with water, lathers like soap. (See also soapwort, page 46.)

Houseleek (*Sempervivum* spp.). The tissue of houseleek retains water, making it a fat plant whose leaves have a fleshy appearance. Often found growing on thatched roofs, it is said to protect houses from lightning. In

July and August, rosettes from the year before give rise to thick stems covered with thorny flowers. Numerous other species exist, some of which are improved for use in rock gardens.

Yellow rattle (*Rhinanthus major*). One of the *Scrophulariaceae*, the yellow rattle grows in fields and sometimes infests arable land. It measures 10 to 16 in (25 to 40 cm) in height, and blooms from June to August. The

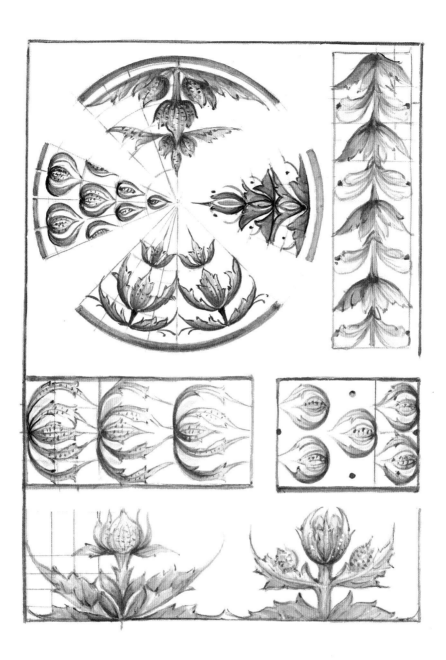

seeds are enclosed in small, dry capsules that rustle in the wind. In the past, this resonant sound signaled the beginning of the hay harvesting season. Yellow rattle is toxic.

Bamboo (*Phyllostachys* spp.). The largest species of grass, bamboo prolif-erates naturally in Asia and forms dense thickets, 10 to 13 ft (3 to 4 m) high. Elsewhere, bamboo is grown to make hedges in gardens: the stalk,

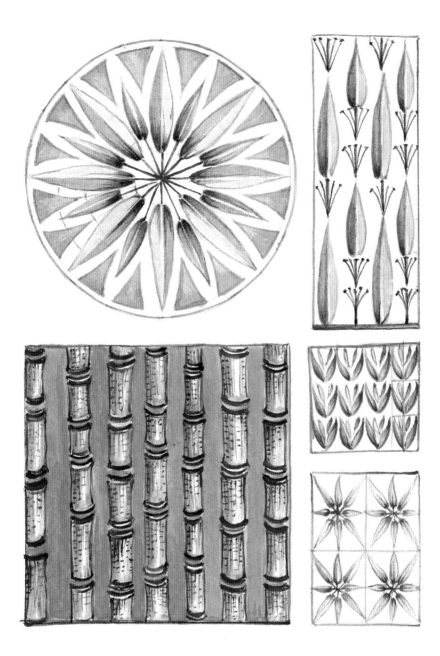

leaves, and shoots are very decorative. If watered frequently, bamboo will
remain green nearly all year long. Dryness gives it a yellowish look and
causes its leaves to fall off.

Cyprus spurge (*Euphorbia cyparissias*). Cyprus comprises a large family of more than 7,000 varieties. They all contain a milky liquid that irritates the skin and is sometimes toxic. Cyprus spurge is also called "wart grass."

It blossoms from May to September and has the reputation of keeping moles away.

Tufted vetch (*Vicia cracca*). Cousin to the pea, this member of the
Papilionoideae family grows along thickets and sunny gullies, decorating
hillsides and hedges from June to August. The veining of its leaves ends

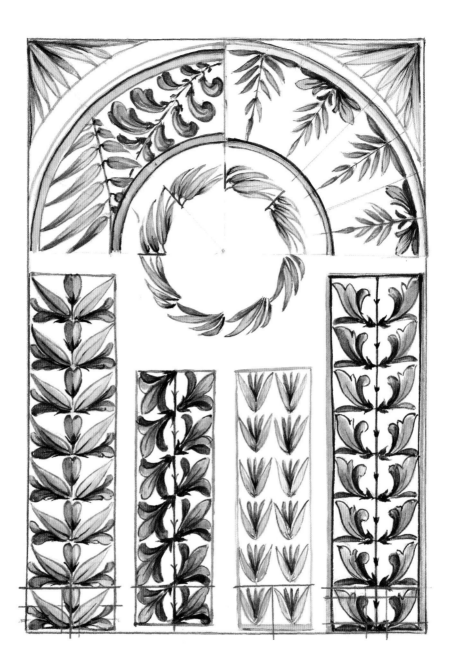

in stipules that allow it to attach itself to the stems of neighboring plants. Vetch is part of a large family, several kinds of which (lucerne, for example) are used as a fodder crop.

Common polypody (*Polypodium vulgare*). Like horsetail, this fern belongs to the very old cryptogam family. Studying its spores and pistils with a magnifier or a microscope can provide good ideas for decoration. Ferns grow especially well on shaded, wet soil. All steps of their development

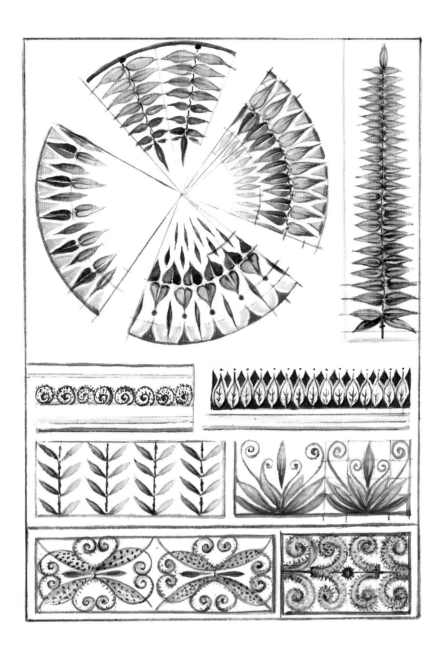

are interesting, from the growth of their new leaves in the spring to the proliferation of their spores, located on the underside of the plant. With its evergreen leaves, the polypody is found even in the winter.

Soapwort (*Saponaria officinalis*). Cousin to the carnation, soapwort grows 12 to 24 in (30 to 60 cm) in height and blooms from June to September. It can be found here and there, near inhabited areas and along roadsides and hedges. It used to be cultivated in gardens for its roots, which contain

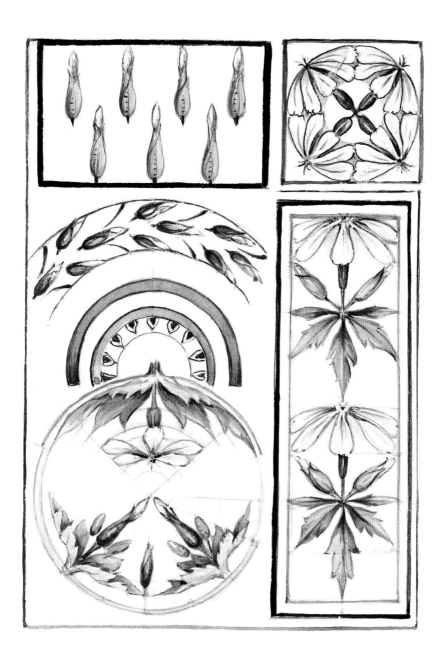

saponin and acts as a lathering agent in water, like soap. It is still used today occasionally for cleaning certain fabric. Soapwort has also enjoyed a reputation for its medicinal uses.

Bull thistle (*Cirsium vulgare*). Bull thistle is a composite plant from an immense family that has inspired me greatly throughout the years. Obviously, the thorns are bothersome, but if you're careful to dig up the plant with a good clump of roots, you can handle it much more easily.

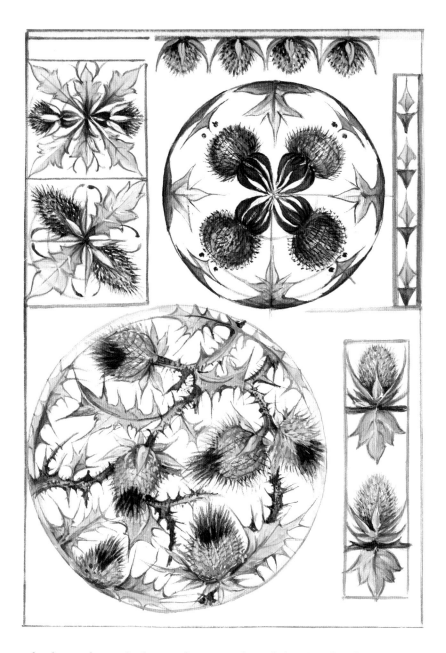

This large plant, which can often exceed 3.3 ft (1 m) in height, grows in chalky soils of meadows and along roadsides, and blooms from July to September.

Bear's breech (*Acantus mollis*). The breech family (*Acantus* means "thorn" in Greek) comprises more than 2,000 species, some of which are cultivated. In the Mediterranean region you can find over thirty wild species. Since Greek antiquity—recall Corinthian and Roman columns—

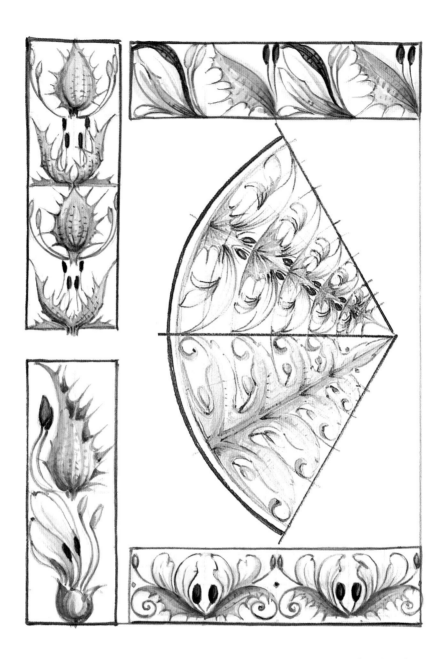

artists have derived inspiration from the leaf of the acanthus family. This beautiful plant measures approximately 3.3 ft (1 m) in height and blooms at the end of spring.

Sea holly (*Eryngium maritimum*). Sea holly is an umbellifer that often takes root in sandy soil near seashores. Reaching 10 to 24 in (25 to 60 cm) in height, its thorny, gray-blue or gray-green leaves give rise to a spherical flower from July to August. Its roots are often put to pharmaceutical use,

as they are praised for their aphrodisiacal virtues. Furthermore, the young leaves are edible and taste rather like cabbage, while the cooked roots have a flavor similar to asparagus.

Borage (*Borago officinalis*). Borage is always at home among other aromatic garden flowers. Reaching a height of 10 to 20 in (25 to 50 cm), it blossoms beautifully from June to October. Bees are attracted to its flowers, which are rich in nectar. Its young leaves and flowers are edible (and

very pretty) in salads. Numerous herbal recipes call for the blue corollas of borage. Originating in the Mediterranean region, this plant gives a pleasant taste to alcohol, and, if you believe in old recipes, it cures the lovesick and comforts the heart.

Wild parsnip (*Pastinaca sativa*). This umbellifer can reach a height of 3.3 ft (1 m) when its double, yellow-gold umbels blossom in July and August along paths and in meadows. It originally comes from southern Europe and was traded in the Middle Ages as a vegetable and medicinal plant.

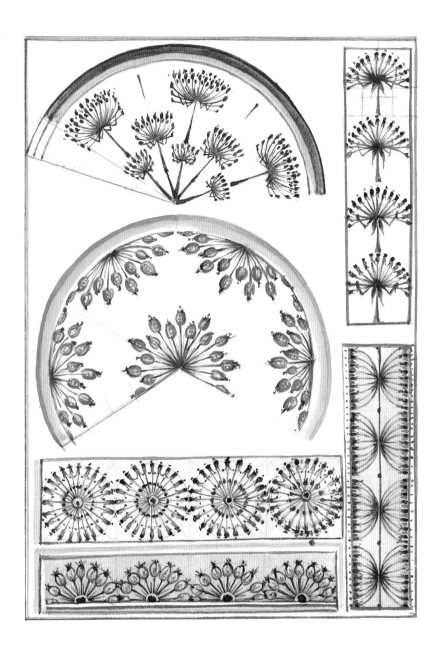

With vitamin-rich roots that can be shredded into salads like carrots, it provides a little extra taste when added to soup. This image was composed in September, when the plant's seeds are tossed around by the wind.

Greater knapweed (*Centaurea scabiosa*). A composite flower able to reach a height of 3.3 ft (1 m), knapweed can be found here and there on hillsides, along roads, and in meadows, where it blossoms from July to

September. It is often confused with its smaller cousin, *Centaurea jacea* (brown knapweed). An ancient remedy against pain and a cough, it is also used as a dye.

Cross-leaved heather (*Erica tetralix*). The dwarf-sized bushes, 4 to 20 in (10 to 50 cm) in height, blossom from July to September in moist, marshy regions. Often used as bedding for animals and fuel for smoking meat,

this plant was also used in certain northern countries to construct roofs and brooms, and smoked in bowl pipes.

Virginia creeper (*Parthenoisissus* spp.). One of the *Ampelidacae*, this is a climbing plant whose leaf, when cut, reveals little crampons and tendrils. Cousin to the grapevine, Virginia creeper is part of a larger family in which the majority of the species are fond of warm climates. Certain

species are cultivated in pots in apartments. Virgin vines decorate the sides of old walls. A deciduous plant, the golden greens, striking reds, and bluish-black fruits of the creeper provide a superb autumn symphony before the onset of winter.

Mountain cranberry (*Vaccinium vitis-idaea*). An evergreen shrub reaching 2 to 12 in (5 to 30 cm) in height, the cranberry belongs to the *Ericaceae* family and blossoms in June. It is common in northern countries on grounds of heather, in woods, and in gardens of moist, acidic soil.

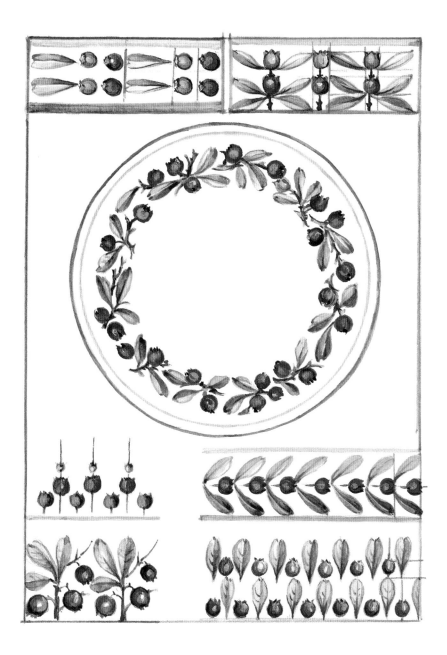

Its white flower resembles that of the cross-leaved heather (see page 60). I am particularly interested in its fruit: ripe from August to September, it can be, after its aesthetic use, transformed into delicious jam; raw, the fruit is rich in vitamins. The leaves are used in refreshing herbal teas.

Blackberry (*Rubus fruticosus*). This thorny member of the *Rosaceae* family, which can reach a height of several feet, blooms from June to September. It can be found in forests, along roadsides, and in thickets. An improved variety, without thorns, can also be found cultivated in gardens.

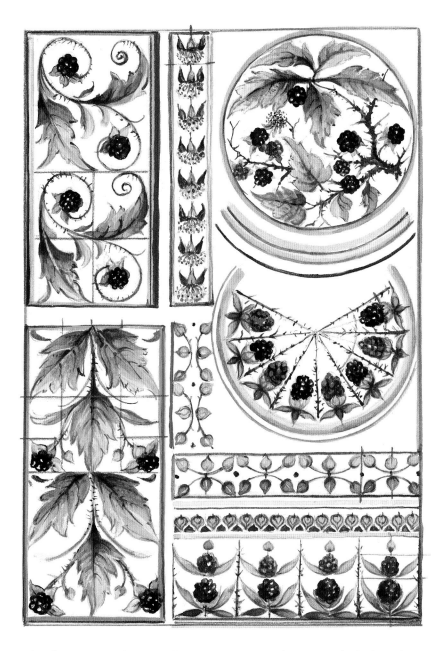

The flowers are white but for several reasons, foremost of which is that they're delicious, it is the fruit of the blackberry bush that I prefer the most. Several other varieties with different tastes exist elsewhere, but they look so much alike, you can't tell them apart. Raspberry is a close relative.

Rugosa rose (*Rosa rugosa*). The rose is, as everyone knows, the queen of all flowers. The wild rose is thorny; it grows up to 9.8 ft (3 m) high and in June and July is covered in white, pink, and violet flowers. In September,

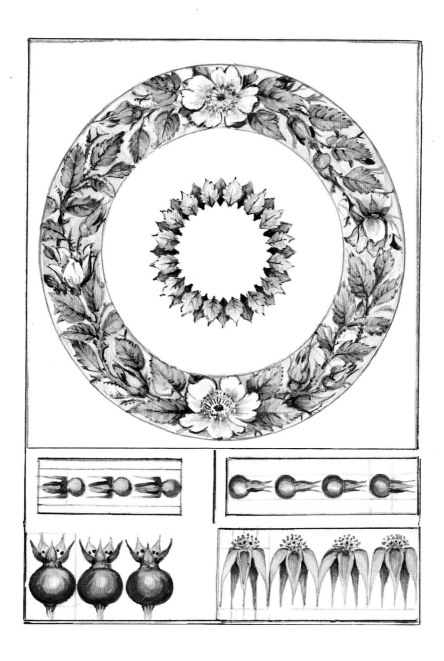

the fruit is ripe; a lovely red-orange and rich in vitamin C, the rose hips are used to make jam. The name corresponds to the "itching powder" of my youth: the berries contain little hairs that make an excellent irritant.

English ivy (*Hedera helix*). All types of ivy are climbing plants with ever-green leaves that grow in moist soils of woods and thickets. They can climb very high—49 ft (15 m)—while attaching themselves to the trunks of trees. Ivy flowers from September to October, but only after eight to

ten years of vegetation. Its flowers are rather insignificant, but the black, globular berries that grow from them are very decorative. Everyone knows ivy's multiple functions in gardens and flower boxes. You can easily propagate ivy in water. It is a toxic plant.

Sea buckthorn (*Hippophae rhamnoides*). A thorny bush that grows 6.6 to 13 ft (2 to 4 m) high, whose sprawling, horizontally growing roots can reach 33 ft (10 m) long, sea buckthorn grows on dunes and hillsides along the sea, particularly in warm, moist, sandy soil. The plant can also be

found in gardens where it is used to create protective hedges and serves as an ornamental bush. It often goes unnoticed when flowering from May to June, but its tangy berries rich in vitamins A and C last until the dead of winter.

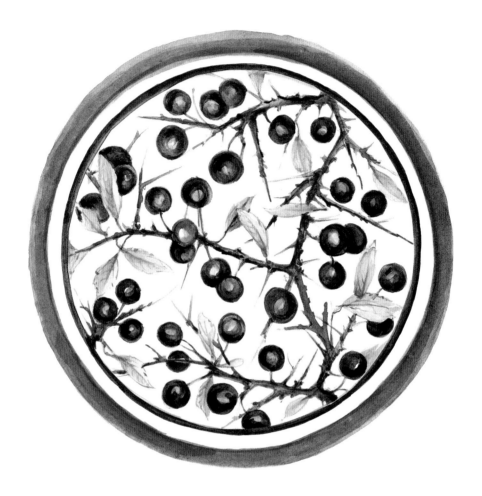

Blackthorn (*Prunus spinosa*). A thorny bush, blackthorn is common in hedges, thickets, and along roads. It flowers nicely in the spring before the leaves of other trees have developed. Who hasn't been tempted by the pungent fruit that ripens at the end of autumn? An excellent liqueur

can be made from the fruit, but you must wait until after the first frost of the season before harvesting them: frost suppresses the acrid taste of the high tannin content.

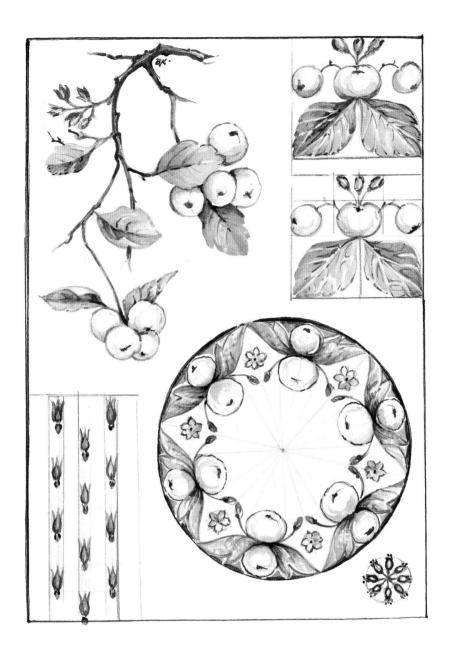

Snowberry (*Symphoricarpus rivularis*). One of the *Caprifoliaceae* that can be found growing wild in North America, snowberry was introduced in Europe around 1800. It is one of the most robust and least demanding of bushes, tolerating shadow and poor soil well. Its small, pink flowers open from May to October, and the white berries illuminate hedges throughout the winter—to the great delight of birds and children—up until the first flowers of springtime appear, and the eternal cycle of vegetation begins again.

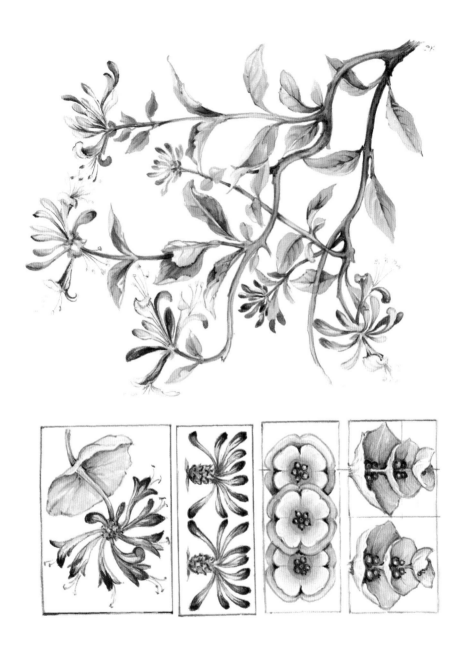

Honeysuckle (*Lonicera* spp.) and woodbine (*Lonicera periclymenum*).

Algae, with a selection of small sea creatures from the Atlantic Ocean.

Chapter Two

Borders
and
Bouquets

This collection of designs is, in a way, a sequel to the first chapter. The forty-three illustrations that follow in this chapter are compositions arranged more or less by seasonal theme, as I conceived them. Captions give a description of each border and bouquet and the plants that compose them.

Christmas Bouquets

You can find green plants for a bouquet even in winter. Here I have used holly (*Ilex aquifolium*) with red berries, mistletoe (*Viscum album*) with light green berries, ivy (*Hedera helix*), and fir tree branches.

Wreath inspired by the bouquet on the previous page.

Left to right: holly border; ivy border; Christmas rose (*Helleborus niger*), which flowers throughout the winter season. The Christmas rose is unrelated to ordinary roses and belongs to the *Ranunculaceae* family.

Springtime Bouquets

Wreath and bouquet of winterling (*Eranthis hiemalis*), snowdrop (*Galanthus nivalis*), alder (*Alnus*), beaked hazel (*Corylus*), and elm flowers (*Ulmus*).

Lungwort (*Pulmonaria officinalis*) border. The flowers of lungwort are initially reddish, but then become dark blue.

Bouquet of corydalis, lungwort, violets (*Viola odorata*), and lesser celandine (*Ranunculus ficaria*).

Oxlip (*Primula elatior*) in a border with lungwort, and in a bouquet with several young beech tree leaves.

Top left: garden violets (*Viola odorata*); top right: coltsfoot (*Tussilago far-fara*); bottom left: wood anemone (*Anemone nemorosa*); bottom right: American liverwort (*Anemone hepatica*).

Wreath of daisies.

Bouquet of Weeds

Dandelion (*Taraxacum vulgare*) border and bouquet of dandelions, violets, and forget-me-nots.

Sea Marsh Bouquet

Border and bouquet of sea pinks (*Armeria maritima*), common vetch (*Vicia angustifolia*), creeping buttercup (*Ranunculus repens*), and grass.

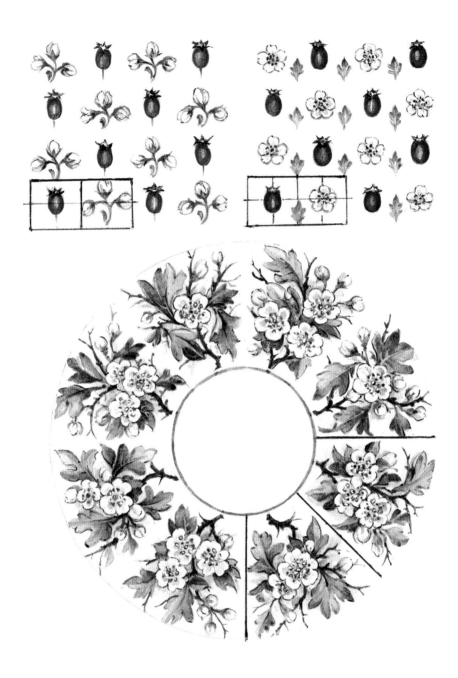

Hawthorn Bouquet

Flowering hawthorn (*Crataegus monogyna*) with red fruit of September.

Apple Blossom Bouquet

Flowers and branches from a wild apple tree (*Malus*).

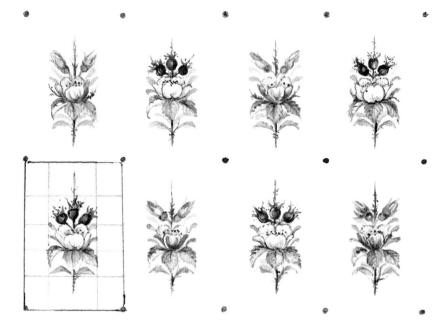

Wild Rose

Border of wild rose; wreath and bouquet of sweetbriar (*Rosa rubiginosa*), Shasta daisy (*Leucanthemum*), and blackcurrant (*Ribes nigrum*).

Dune Bouquet

Burnet rose (*Rosa pimpinellifolia*), sweetbriar (*Rosa rubiginosa*), and tufted vetch (*Vicia cracca*).

Country Bouquets

Borders, wreath, and bouquet of corndaisies (*Chrysanthemum segetum*).

Border, wreath, and bouquet of field poppy (*Papaver rhoeas*), harebell (*Campanula rotundifolia*), and oats (*Avena*).

Garden Flower Wreaths

Nasturtium (*Trapaeolum majus*) and crowberries; pansies (*Viola rafinesquir*).

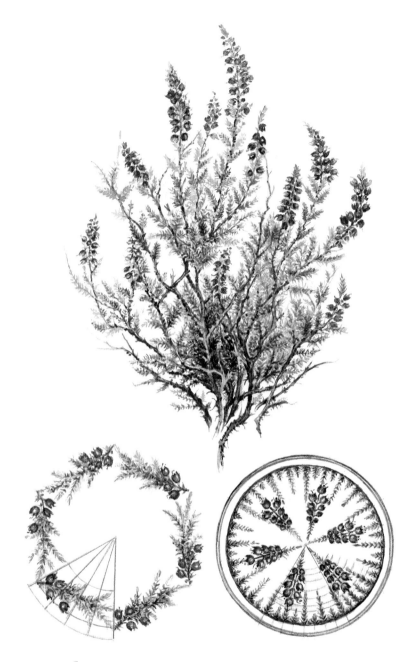

Moor Flower Bouquets

Bouquet and wreath of heather (*Calluna vulgaris*); wreath and border of
crowberries (*Empetrum nigrum*), mountain cranberry (*Vaccinium vitis-*

idea), bilberry (*Vaccinium myrtillus*), cross-leaved heather (*Erica tetral-ix*), common juniper (*Juniperus communis*), and small cranberry (*Vaccinium oxycoccus*).

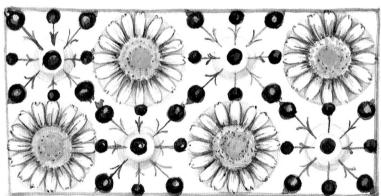

End-of-Summer Bouquet

Borders and bouquet of daisies (*Chrysanthemum leucanthemum*) and blackcurrants (*Ribes nigrum*).

Mushroom Wreath

The mushroom is a rich theme to exploit because of the variety of colors and shapes of its different species.

Autumn Bouquets

Snowberry (*Symphoricarpos rivularis*), wild rose berries, sea buckthorn (*Hippophae rhamnoides*), and beech tree branches.

Border of different types of thistle.

Bouquet with thistle.

Bouquets with thistle.

Summer bouquet with two types of daisy and comfrey (*Symphytum officinale*).

Borders and branch of sunflower.

Artichoke borders.

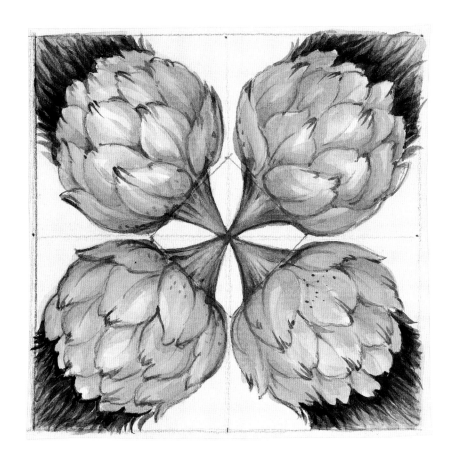

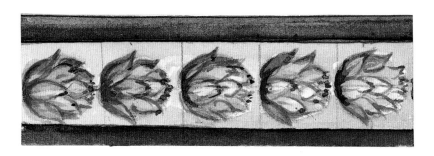

Border and branch of chestnuts.

Tulip border.

Strawberry.

Chapter Three

Folk Art

For the illustrations in chapters 1 and 2 I depended upon plant models. Then I had the desire to do something completely different. The idea of using motifs from folk art came to me very naturally. It is a creative domain that permits one's imagination to run free.

Folkloric ornamentation and decoration have an intriguing history. In studying certain motifs, you come to realize that you can trace their origins through Egyptian and Babylonian civilizations and the earliest cultures (the Indus valley, for example). The same motifs appear in very different geographical contexts. The tulip, for example, is not an ornament unique to Holland, though it has come to be thought particularly Dutch. It actually occurs in the popular art of most European countries.

I choose a motif because it is simple or, on the contrary, marvelously complicated to execute; because I appreciate its symbolism, or because, very simply, I like it. Whatever it may be, the discovery of new motifs offers hours of pleasant research and work. The eighty illustrations in this chapter were inspired by European folklore motifs. The organization is both chronological and geographical.

Crete: Minoan Civilization

Land of the first Europeans, Crete flourished between 2000 and 1400 B.C. The top two figures were inspired by the decorations on a piece of pottery from the Museum of Heraklion; bottom: frieze of wild hens after a fresco mural in the Palace of Cnossos.

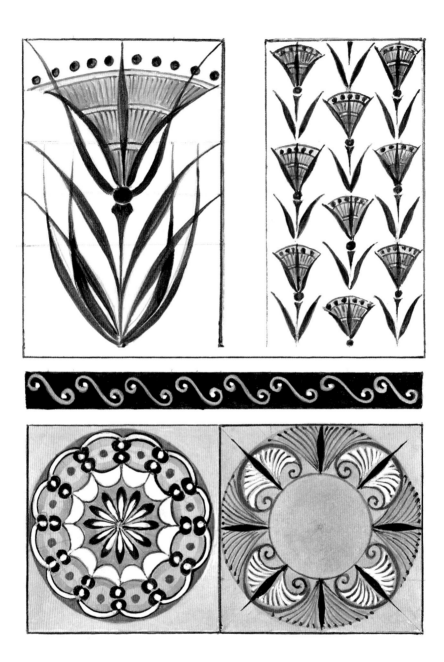

Top: papyrus motif from a piece of pottery; below right: variation on the same motif; bottom left: whimsical ornament on pottery.

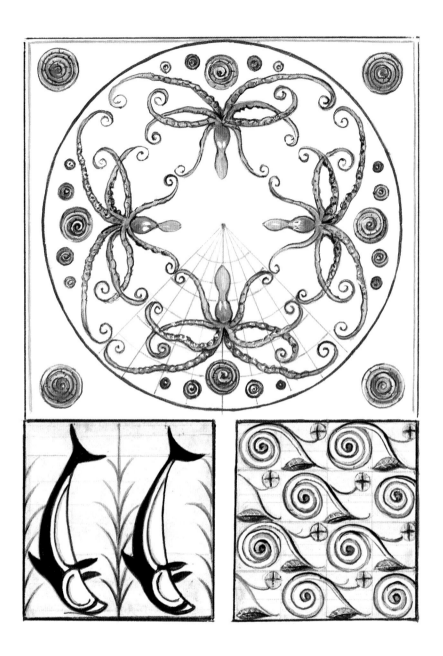

Marine motifs—fish, snails, shellfish, octopus, and waves—are character-istic of this ancient civilization, as are the dolphins jumping through the waves, from a fresco mural. The frescoes are rendered in pastel colors; ceramic decoration is usually dark on a light background.

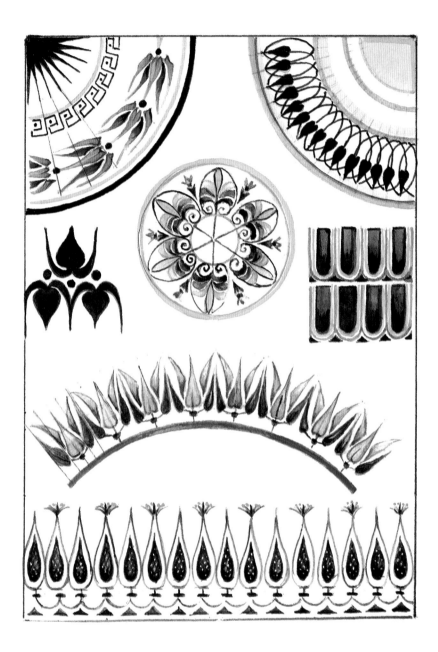

Classical Greece

Top: palmettes. Palmette motifs and lotus flowers often pop up in border compositions. Bottom: seed motif borders, from Greek pottery.

Top: ivy border from the handle on a pitcher; stylized motifs of grazing stags from an Attic pitcher; center left: acanthus and other leaves that decorate Corinthian columns; right: composition of various Greek motifs; bottom left: braid motif from a piece of clothing; bottom right: lotus bud invention (National Museum of Athens).

Etruscan and Roman Civilizations

Friezes from fresco mural in an Etruscan tomb, top to bottom: stylized oval pearls, olive branch, ivy border, palmettes, and fish.

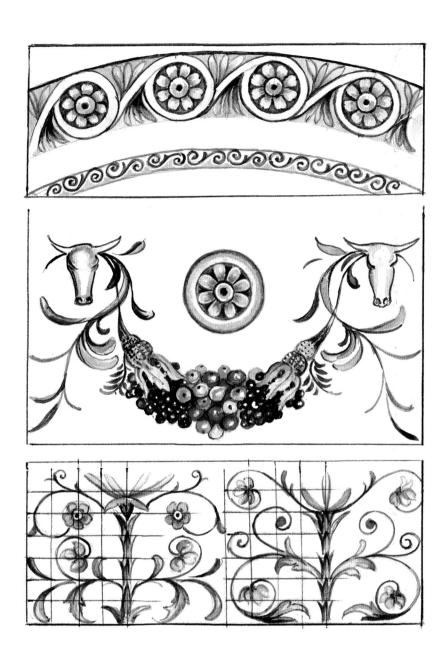

Top: frieze from a marble column; center: cornucopia filled with fruit, hung during celebrations between the heads of animals sacrificed to gods, and detail from a marble altar; bottom: detail of a bas-relief in marble, Altar of the Peace of Emperor Augustus.

Byzantium

Parrot motif, after a ninth-century dish; frame and design at bottom: stylized motif from a column in an archaeological museum in Istanbul.

Top left: plate decoration; top right: composition of palmettes; center: column ornaments; bottom: Pegasus, the winged horse, from a thirteenth-century tapestry (Vatican Museum).

Islam

Islamic popular art periodically exercised influence in southern Europe: a mosaic from Asia Minor.

Top: animals (Asia Minor, thirteenth century); bottom: Iranian-inspired frieze (Victoria and Albert Museum, London).

Turkey

Typically Turkish motifs, influenced by classical Islamic art, from a six-teenth-century plate; bottom left and right: plant motifs.

Top: bird of paradise motif from a plate, ca. 1550 (Victoria and Albert Museum, London); bottom: plant motifs from Islamic art.

Greece

Decorations inspired by borders from the Greek islands, eighteenth and nineteenth centuries (private collection, Athens).

Albania

Designs from the embroidery on a woman's coat, nineteenth century (Okutari).

Bulgaria

From the embroidery of a folkloric suit, nineteenth century (Sofia).

Yugoslavia

Variations inspired by embroidery and leatherwork from Bosnia and Croatia, nineteenth and twentieth centuries (Museum of Sarajevo, Ethnographic Museum of Zagreb).

Italy

Top: composition inspired by floral decoration of majolica, Venice, seventeenth century; center: stylized oval pearls; bottom: border from a piece of pottery (Palermo), seventeenth century and central sun motif from Faenza tile, fifteenth century.

Top: floral ornament on a carafe of Sardinian wine; bottom: Byzantine-inspired birds and oak foliage from a Florentine pitcher, ca. 1450.

Spain

Top: motif from embroidery details on woman's clothing from the region of Carra, Salamanca; bottom: Moorish-inspired motif on a piece of pottery, Granada, eleventh century.

Motifs from embroidery designs on folkloric clothing from the region of Salamanca.

Portugal

Mosaic design from the chapel of Santa Maria of Chamusca, ca. 1700.

Decorations from seventeenth-, eighteenth-, and nineteenth-century
plates (Ethnographic Museum of Lisbon).

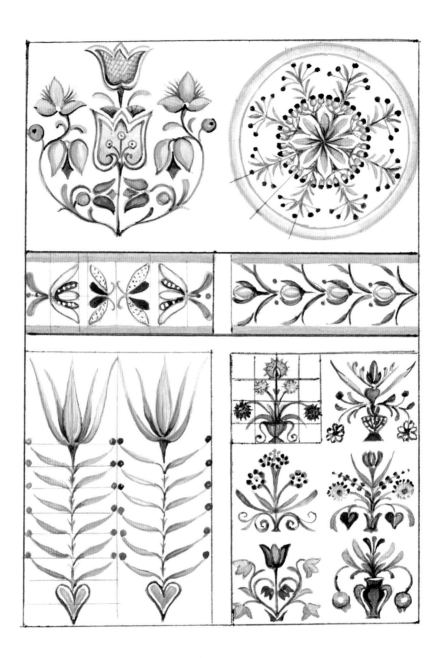

Romania

Motifs inspired by Romanian ceramic tiles of the eighteenth century.

From embroidery and appliqué on a leather vest (Transylvania).

Hungary

Four plates from Sárospatak, northeast Hungary (Tokay), ca. 1900, and an ornament from a carafe of wine, early eighteenth century.

Top: six motifs from different regions of Hungary; center: four motifs from Sárospatak; bottom: small bowl from Sárospatak, ca. 1850.

Czechoslovakia

Composition based on mural paintings, embroidery, and leatherwork from the region of Lanzhot, Mähren, nineteenth century.

Friezes inspired by pieces of pottery and Slovakian plates, nineteenth century (Narodni Museum, Prague).

Austria

Top: border from a carafe of wine, eighteenth century; center: decor from a wooden box, nineteenth century; bottom: details from a carafe of wine, eighteenth century.

Top: after designs on an eighteenth-nineteenth century plate; bottom left and right: details from a wooden box; bottom center: two chamois from a Salzburg powder horn, nineteenth century. Austrian motifs are often conceived symmetrically around a median line. Chamois and stags are very popular motifs in the country.

Switzerland

Borders inspired by paintings on rustic furniture, eighteenth century, Appenzell (Switzerland Folkloric Museum, Zurich); bottom: two motifs from a Heimberg plate, eighteenth century.

Top: details from decorations on rustic furniture, Berne, beginning of eighteenth century; bottom: variations on frieze motifs on preceding page.

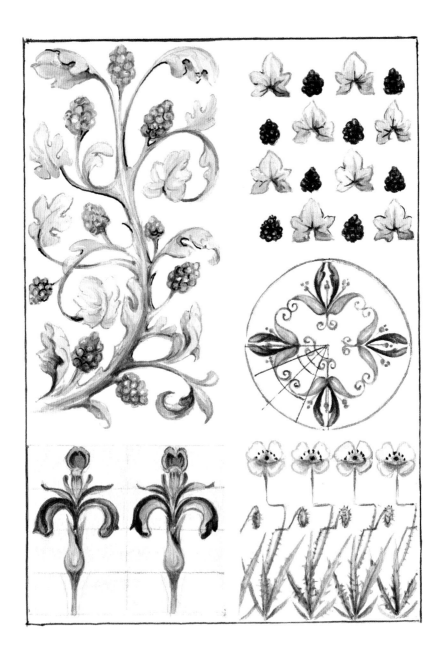

France

Top: Gothic pampres and grapes, from a bas-relief in Notre-Dame, Paris, ca. 1175; bottom: iris, probably the origin of the gothic motif of the fleur de lis emblem of the king of France, and naturalized version of a poppy border, Art Nouveau, 1902.

Design on a jar of ointment, Saint Cloud, eighteenth century (Museum of Decorative Arts, Paris).

Russia

The top five motifs were inspired by tablecloths of shimmering colors from the Votjak region, twentieth century; the borders below by embroidery on a table runner, Ukraine, twentieth century.

Decorative motifs from boxes made of silver birch bark and baskets, nineteenth century, Volgoda region.

Poland

Borders and motifs inspired by plates, bowls, and candlesticks from southern Poland.

Top left: from a dish from the region of Cracow, nineteenth century; top right: from a plate from the region of Stanislavov, nineteenth century; bottom: bird motifs from paper cutouts, nineteenth and twentieth centuries. The paper cutouts were used to decorate walls and windows (National Museum of Varsovie).

Germany

Top left: stag on terra-cotta pottery from Pomerania, eighteenth century; top right: details from a terra-cotta pitcher, Rhine region, nineteenth century; center, left: from a plate, Baden, seventeenth century; center, right: from an embroidery of an eagle with two heads, Vierland, seventeenth century; bottom left: tulips from rustic furniture, Pomerania, eighteenth century; bottom right: motif from a dish, Badischer, Black Forest, nineteenth century.

Top: from a Spreewald tankard, eighteenth-nineteenth centuries; center: from a motif painted on a chest (Amt Neustadt), eighteenth century; bottom, from a motif painted on a Tyrolian chest, Zillertal, North Tyrol.

The following pages present borders from Kellinghusen ceramics, produced in Slesvig-Holstein, nineteenth century. The flat part is generally decorated with flowers or birds in lively colors on a characteristically yellow background.

Kellinghusen bouquet of lilacs.

172

Kellinghusen lemon and berry bouquet.

Kellinghusen blue daisies.

Kellinghusen pink tulip.

Kellinghusen large bird and campanule.

Kellinghusen yellow tulip and berries.

Kellinghusen bouquet with roses.

Holland

Top and bottom left: ornaments inspired by wood engravings from the eighteenth century, Hindeloben; top right: from a basket of flowers on Frisian tile, early nineteenth century; bottom: variation on a three-tulip motif found on numerous Dutch tiles.

Top left: fruit-basket motif inspired by a tile from the seventeenth century; center, left: bird motif, tile from the seventeenth century; bottom left: pomegranate from early seventeenth-century tiles; right: designs on Dutch tiles, among others, three-tulip motif.

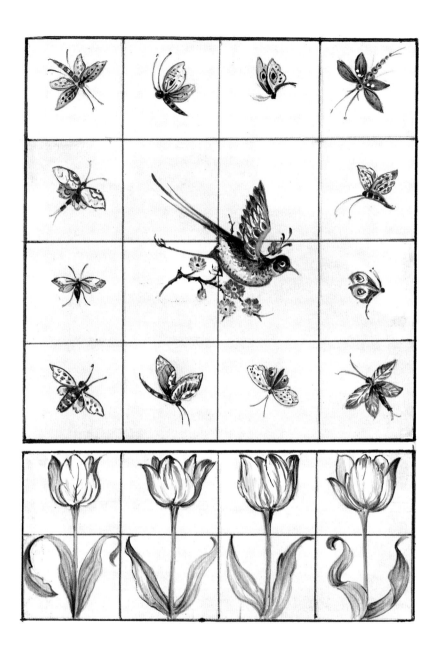

Top: insect and bird details from a painting, *Vase of Flowers,* by De Roos, Delft, ca. 1700; bottom: from tulip tiles, Hoorn, ca. 1640.

Belgium

Top: from a tile floor, fifteenth century, Anvers; bottom: details from a chateau mosaic, Ecouen (Royal Museum of Brussels).

England

Top (both pages): from a tile floor, Keynsham Abby, Somerset, thirteenth-fourteenth centuries; bottom (both pages): motifs inspired by ceramics from the sixteenth and seventeenth centuries (Stoke-on-Trent Museum and Art Gallery)—pomegranates (this page); tulips (opposite).

Celtic Ireland

Top: cross and stars; center: dragons and spirals; bottom: border of doubled hatchets.

Top: intertwining spirals inspired by illustrations in the *Books of Celts*. Figures of three and six concentric circles are very common, as are the intertwined and curling motifs. Bottom: bird ornaments in concentric circles.

Iceland

Viking motifs involving dragons and other mythic animals. Of all the Scandinavian countries, Iceland has the most profound traces of Viking artwork.

Top: from the strap of a drinking flask, eighteenth century; center: from a cane decorated with a ram's horn motif; bottom: from a wooden casket, eighteenth century (National Museum of Reykjavik).

Norway

Rosemaling motifs: traveling painters decorated walls, ceilings, furniture, and everyday objects with rustic rosemaling in the eighteenth and nine-

teenth centuries. The decorations were often executed on a plain green, red, blue, or brown background—"popular" colors—with the help of a large paintbrush covered in several colors at once.

Denmark

Decorations inspired by rustic wooden chests, 1750–1850. The chests
were used primarily to store bedding and clothing. Generally, crowns of

flowers encircled the initials of the owner and the year in which the chest was received. As in Norway, the motifs were painted on a somber background.

Sweden

Bouquets and garlands from paintings of the Zorn Museum of Mora (Dalecarlie). The popular art of this region was largely inspired by biblical illustrations of the eighteenth century. Crude motifs, painted on wood or

paper, reproduced scenes from the Old and New Testaments, but all the figures were clothed in contemporary garments. Borders, like those on the top of the facing page and above, enclosed action scenes into which garlands and baroque bouquets were mixed.

Finland

Top: four decorations inspired by jewelry from the eighth and ninth centuries called "Kalevala," the name of the Finnish national epic; bottom: from a decorated spinning wheel, Österbotten, nineteenth century.

Lapland

Top: two motifs inspired by the knob of a hiking cane; center: triangular, geometric motifs; bottom: motifs inspired by a sculpted, wooden lid. Laplanders are a nomadic ethnic minority who live in northern Norway, Sweden, and Finland. Their tradition of artistry is extremely old. The motifs are designed and engraved with knives on wood, bone, and horns, and decorate everyday objects from skis to wooden buckets.

Chapter Four

"Chinoiserie"

My great-grandfather, Christian Thornam, participated in a worldwide scientific expedition as an animal renderer. In 1847 he brought back, in a multitude of sketches that were assembled into a book, souvenirs of his adventures that constituted a part of the heritage left to our family. At the time he visited, the borders of China and Japan were only partially open; he discovered these countries through what he saw in Singapore, Hong Kong, Macao, Canton, and Shanghai. By "chinoiserie," carefully enclosed in quotation marks, I mean motifs based on these and other Asian sources. Birds and flowers predominate. Old Chinese prints depict many imaginary birds. In China, summer is symbolized by the lotus flower, autumn by the chrysanthemum, winter by cherry or plum tree flowers, and spring by peonies. I have found motifs in classical ceramics, porcelain, and numerous ancient engravings from Asia. Of course, a real knowledge of the varied cultures of the East can be gained only by serious study of the subject. I have tried, however, to indicate my references as well as the approximate origin of my sources of inspiration.

Six vignettes arranged in circles: cherry, butterfly, bird, bindweed, chrysanthemum, and bamboo.

Birds in branches

From a vase painted by Nonomura Ninsei, beginning of the Edo period
(middle of the seventeenth century), Japan.

From a decoration created by the Kakiemon family, end of the seventeenth century, Arita province, Japan.

The phoenix—symbol of the southern world—and flowering branches. A technique from the green family, Kangxi period (ca. 1662–1722), China.

Two pheasants, decoration from the Kakiemon family workshop, seventeenth century, Japan.

Plant inspired from a vase called "The One Hundred Flowers," rose
family, Qianlong era (1736–1795).

Japanese geisha, inspired by a Shigemasa print, ca. 1776.

Chrysanthemum branch, adapted from a punch bowl, end of the eighteenth century.

Adapted from a decoration on a bottle of sake, produced by Nabeshima, early eighteenth century, Japan.

Floral composition adapted from a plate design, Ko Kutani workshop (1660–1694), Japan.

Apricots, adapted from a dish design, Kangxi period (1662–1722), China.

Two decorations from a vase and a dish, Kakiemon workshop, ca. 1700, Japan.

Birds perched on bamboo and flowering trees, Ko Kutani workshop (1660–1694), Japan.

Composition freely adapted from a vase, Qing dynasty, Kangxi period, seventeenth century, China.

Composition from a decoration on a Japanese barber's washbasin, Genroku period (1688–1703), Imari style.

Composition freely adapted from a Chinese pitcher. Rose family, Lady
Wantage, Yongzheng period (1723–1735).

Peonies and magnolias. Decoration from the rose family, Yongzheng period, eighteenth century, China.

Stylized lotus motif from a dish, beginning of the Kakiemon style (1652–1672), Arita province, Japan.

Compositions based on an ancient Japanese print by Hokusaï (1760–1849), master of the art of painting nature. No one "could, like him, reproduce even the smallest leaf as simply, with as much exactitude."

Facing page: heron and duck. Above: cranes in a landscape.

Lotus flowers, Xuande period (1426–1435), China.

Flowering apricot, from a Chinese vase, Kangxi period (1662–1722).

Birds and flowers.

Composition from a motif painted on a water pitcher, Song era, China.

Fish platter, Ming dynasty, China.

Composition inspired by a dish from the green family, Kangxi period (1662–1722), China.

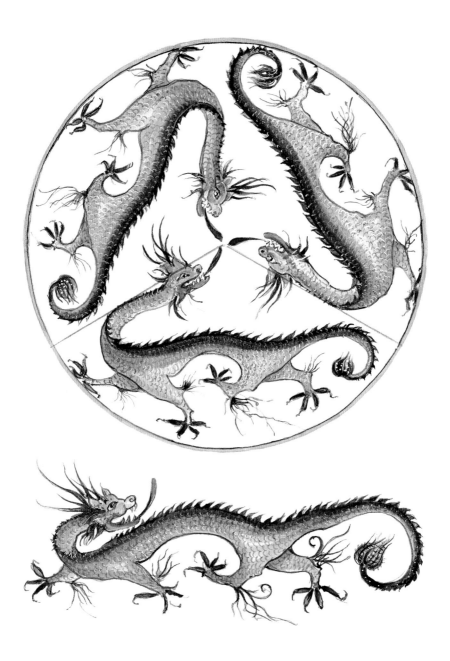

The dragon is a motif often used in Chinese decoration; it is a symbol of fecundity.

Peonies, from a sandstone vase, Song dynasty (960–1279), China.

Decoration adapted from an enameled casket, ca. 1900.

Composition from a lacquered Japanese stand.

Six vignettes with a cherry-blossom motif.

Tiger motif from a sixteenth-century wall painting, Acra, India.

Motifs inspired by silk embroideries, seventeenth century, Rajasthan, India.

Bird motifs from ancient paintings, New Delhi, India.

Designs from a quilt, Coromandel Coast, India.

Bali mask motifs.

Wallpaper designs inspired by shadow puppets, Djakarta, Indonesia.

Motifs inspired by shields, Borneo.

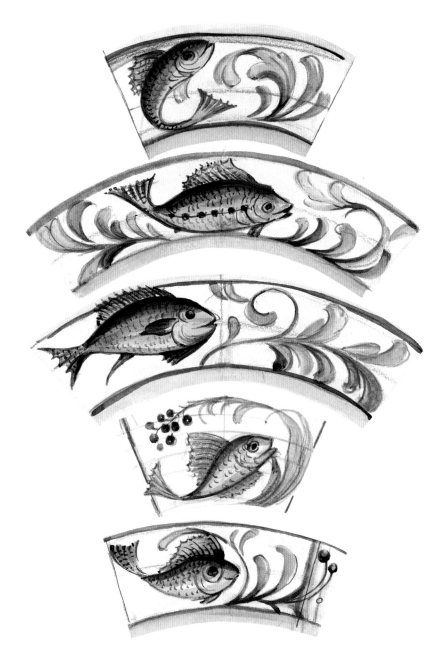

Coral fish, India.

Dragons, Taiwan.

Index